*'I've told you before –
no Samsung phones at
the dinner table'*

THE BEST OF

2017

MATTHEW PRITCHETT
studied at St Martin's School of Art in
London and first saw himself published
in the *New Statesman* during one of its
rare lapses from high seriousness. He has
been the *Daily Telegraph*'s front-page
pocket cartoonist since 1988. In 1995,
1996, 1999, 2005, 2009 and 2013 he
was the winner of the Cartoon Arts Trust
Award and in 1991, 2004 and 2006 he
was 'What the Papers Say' Cartoonist of
the Year. In 1996, 1998, 2000, 2008 and
2009 he was the *UK Press Gazette*
Cartoonist of the Year and in 2015 he
was awarded the Journalists' Charity
Award. In 2002 he received an MBE.

Own your favourite Matt cartoons.
Browse the full range of Matt
cartoons and buy online at
www.telegraph.co.uk/photographs
or call 020 7931 2076.

The Daily Telegraph

THE BEST OF

MATT

2017

An Orion Paperback

First published in Great Britain in 2017 by Orion Books
A division of the Orion Publishing Group Ltd
Carmelite House
50 Victoria Embankment
London
EC4Y 0DZ

A Hachette UK Company

10 9 8 7 6 5 4 3 2 1

A CIP catalogue record for this book is available from the British Library.

ISBN: 978 1 4091 6463 0

Printed in the UK by CPI Group (UK) Ltd, Croydon, CR0 4YY

The Orion Publishing Group's policy is to use papers that are natural,
renewable and recyclable products and made from wood grown in
sustainable forests. The logging and manufacturing processes are
expected to conform to the environmental regulations of the country
of origin.

www.orionbooks.co.uk

'You borrowed Daddy's phone. Try to remember where you moved my bank account to'

THE BEST OF
MATT
2017

'If the UK is destroyed in a nuclear attack, these are the codes for triggering Article 50'

'The uncertainty over Article 50 makes them terribly nervous'

'Two Englishmen in Whitehall.
One says "Which way to Brexit?"
The other one replies
"I wouldn't start from here"'

'The European Court of
Justice demanded to rule
on all line calls'

'Mary Berry will now tell us how to prevent our hard Brexit having a soggy bottom'

'You can be in our gang, but if you want to leave it will take years of negotiation and cost £60bn'

Brexit

'Thank goodness we moved in here after the Brexit vote. Civilisation will have collapsed by now'

Prices increase

'Your Vauxhall is now French.
Will it be allowed to stay
in the UK after Brexit?'

Peugeot buys Vauxhall

'We're from the UK.
We've come to sell you
Cornish pasties and
bagless vacuum cleaners'

Brexit

'Hello, Mrs May. Yes, we have received your letter ...'

'I want to impress Theresa May, so I'm going to stop her coming back into the country'

'Ready? The first to 21 points gets into the country'

Brexit

'Mrs May's Brexit is a little harder than we'd been led to expect'

'This is where we scrap all the EU Health & Safety laws'

'I shall be calling for a
Hokey Cokey Brexit.
One leg in and one leg out'

'I seem to remember my
family motto is "Thwart
the Will of the People"'

'Tony Blair said a second EU referendum was needed because Michael Gove had acquired weapons of mass destruction'

'Our roof voted to leave.
Stop remoaning'

'I'd just turned to my wife
and said "Finally, we're
taking back control"'

'Today I'm discussing the future of Brexit with experts who all got the election result wrong'

'Our son's an EU citizen who has been here more than five years – we can't get rid of him'

'Prime Minister, the Brexit bill is €100bn and the EU wants to know if you'd like to add a tip'

'If they offer us coffee, hold out for biscuits as well'

Corbyn

'Do you ever walk into a room and find you've completely forgotten whether you're in the shadow cabinet?'

'I used to be a Labour whip, so herding cats is a piece of cake'

Hired and fired

'He spent 20 minutes telling me what a disaster Corbyn would be. I assume he's the Labour candidate'

'Leaked? Even the one about coveting your neighbour's ox?'

'That's not an internet ransom demand. That's the Labour manifesto'

Labour Manifesto leaked

'Diane Abbott has committed Labour to spending roughly this much on policing'

Figures confusion

'I want a strong coffee.
A strong and stable coffee.
Not a weak coffee, propped up
by a coalition of chaos'

'The Lib Dem manifesto
was leaked to us last
week, but nobody could
be bothered to read it'

'It's about your social care. I'm
a little concerned about
the results we've had back
from your estate agent'

'The polls are narrowing.
Now is the time for
strong, stable panicking'

Social care blunder

'My dad's an opinion pollster.
I hope he never loses that sense
of wonder and surprise
at election results'

'I'm just going to stay up
until someone eats
Paddy Ashdown's hat'

'It turns out the voters are
bloody difficult as well'

'Hello, I recently bought a
strong and stable dining
table from you ...'

'Vince Cable is 74. By the time of the next election he could be 74 and a half'

'That's not the Queen. That's how the DUP travels these days'

'There's a vote on the Queen's Speech. Can we take out the ten DUP MPs?'

Billion pounds for DUP

'The Queen will deliver
her speech by speakerphone
from Ascot'

Queen's Speech delayed

'Get the Rolls out,
I'm going on a Day of Rage'

Austerity over

UKIP

'The party is divided.
The loonies may split
from the fruitcakes'

'Wonderful. I'd rate that as one
of Nigel's top three resignation
speeches of all time'

'I'm very fastidious.
I change my socks every
time UKIP changes leader'

'This infighting is terrible.
Thank goodness we don't
have two MPs'

'*Amazing. One day we'll be able to tell our grandchildren about this – I hope*'

'Mrs May was the tenth leader
to speak to Donald Trump,
but the first to receive a
smiley face emoji'

'Darling, the UK has been a
fool. America has been having
a special relationship with
Germany all along'

'We have agents who will risk their lives, infiltrate Isil or spy on the Russians, but none who were prepared to listen in on Donald Trump'

'Oh Covfefe!'

Mysterious tweet

'Never mind the cherry tree.
You're hereby terminated,
effective immediately, Father'

'Don't tell me what happens.
I'm waiting for the film'

Trump fires FBI director

'If you want to have your brother killed you may have to become leader of North Korea'

HINKLEY POINT

'The Chinese insisted on them'

'The captain has sighted the
Russian navy. England
expects every passenger
to do their duty'

Russian fleet sails through
Channel

'Santa knows if you've been
good or naughty because
Putin tells him everything'

'I don't want to be president of France if it means I have to marry my teacher'

'You must remove the socks from under your sandals'

'The manager's brought
shame on English football.
That's the players' job'

'He leaves with an unblemished
record – played one, won one'

'We played football at school. In here is my dirty kit and £100,000. Don't ask'

'Can Johnny come out and make a speech in the Far East for £55,000?'

'Look away now if you don't want to know the size of the bung your club manager received'

'Oi, REF!!! You're the only principled, decent man in the whole game'

'...or, for an extra £50,
you can play in midfield'

'GO ON, SON...FOUL HIM...
BRIBE THEM...
GIVE HIM A BUNG'

Rail Delays

SOUTHERN

CANCELLED	CANCEL
CANCELLED	CANCEL
CANCELLED	CANCEL
CANCELLED	CANCE

'Will I be home before the
UK has left the EU?'

THE (SOUTHERN)
RAILWAY CHILDREN

'Do you think it will
be here soon?'

'The Government would
like to offer you the
Southern Rail franchise'

'We've found these all over southern England. We have no idea what they're for'

'The strikes forced me to work from home. I'm having a drink with colleagues'

'How infuriating! The rail company didn't tell me about the cheaper options'

NHS

'Your cheque bounced. We're going to have to put your appendix back'

'Sorry, I should have made myself clearer. It's your PASSPORT that expires in one month'

NHS Tourism

'We've started using leeches
again. They don't make you
better, but they're happy to
work at weekends'

'There are four seasons: Winter
NHS crisis, Spring NHS crisis,
Summer NHS crisis and
Autumn NHS crisis'

'If we can't get our children
into the best schools by buying
houses in the catchment areas,
what will we talk about?'

GRAMMAR
SCHOOL

ENTRANCE
EXAM

'If a triangle has one side of
3cm and another of 4cm,
how many private
tutors did your parents hire?'

'Many of our pupils go on to have successful careers opposing selective schools'

'We've diversified. We're now a pub and grammar school'

'I'm self-employed, so the Budget was a nasty surprise'

'Robin suggested taking from the self-employed and the men became less merry'

Unpopular Budget

'The new business rates
forced us to move
to smaller premises'

'I've just invented
business rates!'

Budget

'Everything is disposable these days. I remember when a Budget would last nearly 48 hours'

'This is the last spring Budget U-turn. From now on, Budget U-turns will be in the autumn'

'He said he wanted to spend more time with his family, if he could remember which pub he left them in'

'The Camerons' daughter had a party and peerages were the going home presents'

Independence Referendum 2

'Not tonight. The thought
of a second Scottish
referendum has given
me a terrible headache'

'Let's forget our differences
over Brexit and fall out over
independence instead'

'Dads, there's something
I have to tell you: I want
to be an Anglican bishop'

'There was a mix up and
I married the vicar
instead of my fiancée'

The Royals

'Any chance of a tea with four sugars, Ma'am?'

Palace Restoration

Philip retires

'Control tower to Zac Goldsmith: you're cleared for flounce off'

'We can't build a runway here. It would disturb an extremely rare Lib Dem MP living nearby'

Olympics

'It's the ultimate test. He has to excel in four separate disciplines: sitting, watching, eating and drinking'

'Nobody move! This is worse than a lost contact lens. I've dropped Tom Daley's swimming trunks'

'That's what happened when a mosquito bit a Russian athlete'

'This vaccine is from Russia. A possible side effect is that you could run 100m in under 10 seconds'

'Don't worry, Bake Off can't actually leave the BBC till Theresa May has triggered Article 50 ...'

'Bad news, we've only got one half of the double entendres'

'I thought while we're waiting
I'd try to grow some courgettes'

Oscars

*'I enjoyed it, but I didn't think
the end was very believable'*

*'Is he slipping on the ice
or doing the dance
from La La Land?'*

Wrong envelope

And finally...

'And now my male colleague will read the Autocue more expensively'

BBC gender pay gap

'After the stork delivered me, did it go home and sext another stork?'

'Great news, the baby on
our flight has grown up
and stopped crying'

BA computer crash

'If you take away my son's
iPad he might "go off"
during the flight'

And finally...

And finally…

'This tribute to the fallen –
what's in it for us?'

'We'd like to have the team's
mascot put down'

Claudio Ranieri sacked

'You've been asleep for 100 years. I have bad news about the money you left in your savings account'

'It's closed, but the queue seems to be moving faster than when it's open'

And finally...

'Well at least fracking has solved our mole problem'

'DRY JANUARY? This is muddled thinking which is bound to end in failure!'

'I'm your doctor. I didn't study
medicine, but I was born
within the sound of Bow bells'

UK doctors debate

'I'm taking this with me
in case I have an accident
and end up in A&E'

And finally...

'When you have your hair done do you give the person who washes it an MBE, or just the stylist?'

'Johnnie Johnson is in here. The plan is to bounce him through a window of Buckingham Palace when they give out knighthoods'

Honours

'Nobody WANTS to be King of the Jungle, it's just a duty'

'We need a chairman who is well-informed about drugs and prostitution – but not an expert'

And finally...

Keith Vaz resigns

And finally...

'Welcome to Just a Minute. In our new version, Ken Livingstone will attempt to talk for 60 seconds without mentioning Adolf Hitler'

'I had a sex robot, but it ran off with the fridge'

'North Korea acquires
Whirlpool tumble dryers'

'This is the navy's latest sub.
It's armed with lethal,
over-cooked roast potatoes'

Health scare

'I'm Poldark body ready'

'The bad news is Europe has backed the headscarf ban. The good news is we've been accepted by Muirfield golf club'

'It's very economical. You can drive from the showroom to the scrappage centre on one tank of fuel'

And finally...

'I had no idea the
Duke of Westminster
owned all this as well'